Tango

FOR

P I A N O

PLAYED BY FEDERICO MIZRAHI

Cover Layout by Eric Peterson
Layout by David Collins
Cover Photo courtesy of Yolanda Rossi & Micheal Espinoza
Tango Instructors and Performers
www.tangosplash.com www.tangoelegant.com

ISBN-13: 978-1-57424-206-5
ISBN-10: 1-57424-204-0
SAN-683-8022

© 2006 Centerstream Publication LLC.
P.O. Box 17878 - Anaheim Hills, CA 92817

Contents & CD Track List

 All the tunes were composed by Jorge Polanuer
Corrected by David Cantoni.
The author wishes to acknowledge the valuable contributions of:
Mónica Cabouli, David Cantoni, José Maria D'ángelo,
Verónica Galdieri and Leonardo Suarez.

Federico Mizrahi

Born in Buenos Aires, Argentina, in 1964, Federico Mizrahi studied piano with Violeta Gainza, Jorge Fontenla and Alicia Dubrovsky, and harmony, composition and style with Prof. Sergio Hualpa. From the start, his musical activity has been linked to the theater, musical comedies, and nightclubs, and particularly to the works of the great playwrighte Bertolt Brecht; in collaboration with Kurt Weild, Mr. Mizrahi directed the musical scores of "Happy Ending" and "The Two-Penny opera", and arranged and recorded "The Small Mahogany, all of these with Suarez Marzal.

Under the direction of Manuel Iedvabni, he was the pianist and arranger of "Contra la Seducción", and he composed and arranged the music for "La buena persona de Se-Chuan". He also composed the music for "Tres Mañanas", which received the **Premio "Pepino el 88"** awarded by the Secretariat of Culture to best theater music and "Chejov Chejova" that received the **ACE 1997 Prize and the Trinidad Guevara Prize** of the Secretariat of Culture of the Buenos Aires Governmment in the same category.

Upon the request of Daniel Marcove, Mr. Mizrahi provided the music for "Bar Ada", also considered when he was granted the **ACE 1997 Award,** the most prestigious theater award in Argentina. His performance in musical comedies includes his performance in "Arrancame la Vida", by Betty Gambartes and Chico Novarro, in which he was musical director and arranger, and on-stage piano player. This show won the ACE Award to the best musical comedy in 1992, and was nominated for best record in 1996. Pianist, arranger, and musical director of Daniel Suarez Marzal's "Brech-Tango", in collaboration with Daniel Suarez Marzal and Luis Longhi.

In January 1999, these artists performed "Borges-Brecht-Tango"at the Teatro de la Maestranza in Seville, Spain. A two-month stint at the Lucernaire Teatre in Paris, performing the show "Tango Chejoviano" directed by Iedvabni ensued. In mid-June of that year, he was arranger and performer alongside Luis Longhi in the show "Demolishing Tangos" which was played for the first time ever at the Paris University Campus. He arranged and was musical director of the criolla operetta "What Laura's love has cost", by Alejandro Dolina, recorded on CD by the National Symphonic Orchestra, and in which important performers, including Joan Manuel Serrat, Mercedes Sosa, Les Luthiers, Jorge Sabato, took part.

The operetta was subsequently performed at the important Teatro Avenida and Teatro Argentino de La Plata of Argentina in 2000. He wrote the original score for the play "El pasajero del barco del sol" written by O. Dragun and directed by Ruben Pires at the Teatro Nacional Cervantes (1999) In 2001, he composed the soundtrack for the theater play "El Pelele" and in 2002 the soundtrack for "La venganza de don Mendo" for the Teatro Municipal Gral San Martín. He has recently been called upon by the Spanish film director Pilar Távora to compose the soundtracks for the films "Tatuaje" and "La puerta de los sueños".

Jorge Polanuer

Saxophone player, Flutist, Composer, Arranger, and Teacher

Received his degree as Flute Professor in 1983 at the Conservatorio Nacional de "Música Carlos Lopez Buchardo", the most prestigious institution in Argentina. He has been a member of the musical-theater group Cuatro Vientos (http://www.cuatrovientos.com.ar) since 1987. With this group, he participated in numerous international festivals, including Madrid, Lisbon, Miami, Caracas, San José de Costa Rica, and Porto Alegre, and recorded five CDs in which other renowned performers have participated: Les Luthiers, Andrés Calamaro, Chango Spasiuk, and Bob Telson.

Prior to co-founding Cuatro Vientos, he took part in various Jazz, Fusion, Classical Music, and Rock groups, among them "Los Abuelos de la Nada", and Andrés Calamaro's band, with whom he recorded four CDs.

Jorge has also composed the music for several theater plays: "Gala", "Shakespeare's Merry Women", "Shakespiriando", "Sinvergüenzas" (No shame), "Cuatro Vientos y el Saxo Mágico" (Cuatro Vientos and the magic sax), "Alma de Saxofón" (Saxophone Soul), and "La Tempestad" (The Storm). Available on CD. He won the "Premio ACE (Asoc. Cronistas del Espectáculo) 2000" (the most important music award in Argentina) on best original music for theater. Also, he published several books for saxophone: "SAXOPHONE STYLES",
"TANGO SOLOS FOR SAXOPHONE".

Jorge Polanuer can be reached at:
Castillo 44 dto 2
Capital Federal (1414) Buenos Aires Argentina
Tel: (5411) 4856-2133
e-mail: jorge@cuatrovientos.com.ar
http://www.cuatrovientos.com.ar

Teaching Argentine Tango

*From the book "Modern Dancing", chapter V, by Mr. and Mrs. Castle Vernon.
New York, 1914*

The Tango is not, as commonly believed, of South American origin. It is an old gipsy dance which came to Argentina by the way of Spain, where in all probability it became invested with certain features of the old Moorish dances. The Argentines adopted the dance, eliminating some of its reckless gipsy traits, and added to it a certain languid indolence peculiar to their temperament.

After Paris had taken the dance up a few years ago, its too sensuous character was gradually toned down, and from a rather obscene exhibition, which is still indulged in by certain cabaret performers, it bloomed forth a polished and extremely fascinating dance, which has not had its equal in rhythmical allurement since the days of the Minuet. Beyond doubt, the Tango correctly practiced is the essence of the modern soul of dancing, the autocrat of the up-to-date "soiree dansant". For it is not only a dance, it is a style; to master the Tango one must first master its style, absorb its atmosphere.

Among the many points in its favour, not the least is this: that it not only commands grace, and especially repose, but it develops and even creates these endowments. The only drawback in America to this lovely dance lies in the fact that nearly all teachers teach it differently. A variety of steps which do not belong to the dance at all nor to the ballroom, for that matter-have been taught and practiced by inefficient teachers. In order to give the dance the absolute popularity it deserves it must be "standardized".

The Argentine Tango is unquestionably the most difficult of the new dances. Perhaps that is why some people still maintain that they "do not like it". Others, never having seen it, declare it "shocking". On broad general principles it is human to disapprove of that which is beyond our understanding or ability. We like best the games we play best. And so for a long time society looked askance upon the Tango. Here and there in the corners of ballrooms one saw a few hardy couples tripping a tentative measure. But usually as soon as the music slides into the wailing, seductive notes of the South American dance everybody developed a sudden interest in supper! Moreover, it was rumored that the Argentine Tango was composed of one hundred and sixty different steps. Enough to terrify the most inveterate dancer.

There may be one hundred and sixty different Tango steps, but I doubt it. I have never seen so many, and Mrs. Castle and I do not dance anything like that number. For the average ballroom Tango a knowledge of six fundamental steps is quite enough. One may work out variations of these. But you will find that when you once have mastered the Cortez, the Media Luna, the Scissors, the Promenade, and the Eight Step you can dance with any exponent of the Tango you are apt to meet.

Nor is the Tango as difficult as it was at first supposed. More difficult than the old-fashioned Two Step, yes. Certainly more difficult than the One Step. But once you get into the swing and rhythm of music more alluring than a Viennese Waltz – well, you are lost. You have become a Tango enthusiast. Personally I believe the Tango and the Maxixe Bresilienne are the dances of tomorrow. The Maxixe is described in the next chapter. More and more people are becoming proficient in the variations of both these South American dances. In the smart ballrooms of New York, London and Paris the One Step and the Hesitation Waltz lead the dances this season. Next season it will be the Tango and the Maxixe.

I would like to add a word of warning to those who take lessons in the Tango, and that is: Take your lessons, if possible, from some one who has danced professionally in Paris, because there are so many good dancers there that anybody who can dance the Tango (and get paid for it) in Paris must really be a good dancer. American teachers go abroad for a few weeks, take a few lessons in the "Abaye" or some of the other places which live on the American tourist, come back home, and, having forgotten all they learned coming over, start in teaching. There are others who go to one of our seaside towns, such as Narragansett, and read of a new dance and begin teaching it. There is, unfortunately, no way of stopping these people. You can only pay your twenty-five dollars an hour. If you don't learn the dance, you get a little exercise and a lot of experience.

The most important thing about the Tango is its tempo. You must, before you can dance at all, understand and appreciate the music, and the best way to learn this is to walk (with or without a partner) in time to it. By doing this you impress upon yourself that it is a slow dance, and that it should be simple, and not full of jerky and complicated steps.

This walking to Tango time is not as easy as it may seem; it should be practiced frequently, so as to make it smooth. The shoulders must not go up and down, the body must glide along all the time without any stops. It is correct wither to walk on your heel and toe or just on the ball of the foot; but the Argentines nearly all seem to walk flat-foot, or else they step out on their heel first. I advise dancers to do what is the easiest for them, for when one is walking comfortably it is easier to do the steps naturally. The first step to master, and one of the most difficult, is the Cortez.

The Cortez

Let us suppose that the gentleman is walking backward and the lady forward (the position is exactly the same as in the commencement of all the dances I have explained so far). Now when you are ready to do the Cortez you pause for two counts on the left foot, which should be in the position shown here. Now the right foot passes back of the left for one count. The left shifts to the side a few inches for one count, and the right does the same thing for one count (keeping behind the left). Thus five counts have been occupied, and the feet should have shifted to the music in this way, provided, of course, that the music is very simple.

The lady's part of this step is, of course, just the opposite. She pauses for two counts on her right foot, going forward, her feet following the gentleman's as closely as possible treading on him.

You must not be discouraged over this step. It is very difficult to do smoothly, and you will not get it without a great deal of patience and trouble. Indeed, many good dancers have never mastered it at all, and probably never will. But that is because they do not appreciate its difficulty or are unwilling to give the necessary time to the step. It can be done, and done well, by any one has patience enough to learn it. To get it perfect you should do several steps of the Cortez and then walk, and they go back again into the Cortez. If you can do this you have practically mastered the Tango Argentine.

The Promenade

The position is the same as in the figure eight of the One Step. The man, who should be walking forward, turns the lady so that she is facing in the same direction as himself. They then walk forward, the man with his left and the lady with her right, one, two and three. On the "and" the man steps forward on his left heel, and on the third count the right foot shifts forward to the back of the left heel, taking the weight, so you see there are really four steps to three counts like this one, two, and three; left foot, right, left-right. This step can be repeated as many times as desired.

Media Luna

This step is practically a double Cortez. The man steps forward with his right foot, holding it two counts. The left slides forward one count, and the right takes the weight for one count; thus four counts, have been occupied. The man then steps back with his left, holding it two counts; the right slides back one count, and the left takes the weight for one count. The complete step itself occupies eight counts, but to get the effect the dancers must keep in mind that it must be done smoothly and easily. The position is the same as in the Cortez. The lady's step is, of course, just the opposite. She steps back left, holding it two counts, and then slides the right back one count; the left takes the weight for one count, repeating the step forward with the right.

Scissors

The dancers promenade once, and instead of continuing forward with the outside foot they do a half-turn inward –that is, the man crosses the left in front of the right; now they do the Promenade Step, the man with the right turning inward, crossing the right in front of the left. This can be done as often as desired and can be finished with the Cortez or by continuing the Promenade. It is rather difficult to explain, but the photographs should convey the meaning.

El Charon

This step is begun with a Cortez. The man turns the lady so that she walks backward three straight steps, the man going forward three straight steps at the right side of the lady. Keeping this position, the man walks backward three straight steps, the lady going forward, the man goes forward, etc., as many times as desired, turning to the left as much as possible. They finish the step by the man leading the lady into the Cortez step.

The Ring

This is a very pretty step in the Tango. The best way to go into it is from the Promenade. The gentleman stands still and crosses the right foot over the left, having the weight of the body equally distributed on both feet. The lady does a Single Step (just like the Single Step in the Maxixe) right around the gentleman. This will, of course, turn the man around, and in doing so uncross his feet; when this is done the lady puts her right foot slowly forward and the man his left foot slowly back, and they go into the Cortez. By practicing this step well you will find it quite possible for the lady to make a complete ring around the gentleman, but it depends greatly on his balance, and if he finds his feet getting wound up again all he has to do is to lift the left foot up and place it at the back for the Cortez. Care should be taken to go into and out of this step very slowly, easily and deliberately.

Tango Volta

This is simply an ordinary Waltz step done very slowly in time to the music, one step to each count left, right, left, and right, left, right; it is a very important and useful step, and should be used to fill in between the more difficult steps.

The Eight Step

The Eight Step has already been explained in the chapter on the One Step.   In the Tango it is exactly the same except that instead of the dancers looking over their elbows, as in the One Step, they remain as much as possible facing each other, and the knees area trifle more bent, which gives a slight up-and-down motion to the walk very similar to a very modified Cake Walk. This is important, because it is only done when the dancers are doing plain walking steps, and so when the lady feels her partner doing this slight "Cake Walk" she knows, or should know, that he is going to do plain steps, and not Cortez or fancy steps. In this, as in all Tango steps, the knees must be kept as close together as possible; don't try to take big strides; the charm of the Argentine Tango lies in its apparent simplicity.

The Innovation

The much talked of Innovation is nothing more or less than the Tango lanced without touching your partner. This is naturally very difficult, and can only be done by good dancers. However, a word of advice may help those who would include it in their repertoire. First of all, the man must learn to lead with his whole body; by this I mean he must convey his steps and direction to his partner by means of head, eyes, and feet. The steps should be broader and more deliberate, and the dancers should travel at the same pace all the time. If by any chance the lady does not follow, and goes into the wrong step, don't stop dancing, but get as closely together as possible, and the man must do a plain walk backward.

When both are ready the man must try to convey the step in a better way. If, when mistakes happen, you keep on dancing, in nine cases out of ten no one will know about it but yourself. On the other hand, no one can miss your mistake if you get confused and stop. The lady should not look at a man's feet in this Innovation, but rather try to get a general view of her partner, so that she may see what he is doing without actually scrutinizing the steps. The hands may be either kept behind your back, on your hips, or in your pockets, look at yourself in a mirror and decide which position suits you best.

1920's Tango Sheet Music

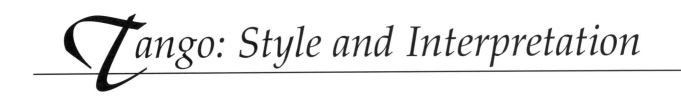

Tango: Style and Interpretation

Popular music is part of the tradition transmitted by word of mouth from generation to generation; for that reason, we do not have a formal methodology for teaching tango; and most of the times, old recordings are the only real source for learning that we have. Although tango is mainly written, it is difficult to find original arrangements or transcriptions. Besides, as it happens with popular music in general, tango is written in a way but played differently. For this reason, it is essential to have some previous stylistic considerations, in order to perform the right execution. It is necessary to observe that one of the most particular thing as ACCOMPANIMENT refers; it is the alternation and use of multiple resources that, in an interaction with the MELODY, give the RHYTHM of TANGO.

It is important to keep in mind that RHYTHM not only comes from the ACCOMPANIMENT, but from the complementation between it and the MELODY, using the infinity of rhythmic and melodic resources that TANGO has, according to what the MELODY "seems to be needing". Therefore, using so varied and changing resources, it is difficult to establish fixed patterns for the ACCOMPANIMENT. As every tango is unique, it is necessary to make a different ACCOMPANIMENT for each one.

It is known that, in general, the parts for Piano that we have are only the notes for the MELODY, with no phrasing or accents, together with an ACCOMPANIMENT that works mainly as a tonal guide or reference; but this is not enough for a good execution of the tune. Hence, a lot of talented musicians, not having a good arrangement, face the impossibility of performing a piece of TANGO with its typical sound.

To play the present versions it should be kept in mind the correct execution of ligatures, accents, staccato, the times when one hand plays legato and the other one staccato, etc. It is advisable, for beginners, to study the parts of both hands separately, in order to be sure of what each of them should play. This practice confers clarity and security when playing with both hands at the same time.

It is essential while performing tango, the alternation between legato and staccato passages; the latter ones, as they confer the authentic tango sound to the execution, should be played whenever is possible. We sometimes listen to versions which having no staccato passages become mere executions of Melody, and although well harmonized, they lose their distinctive sound. These are general indications and there may be exceptions to them.

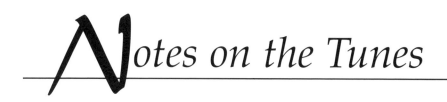otes on the Tunes

1. The Handkerchief *(Tango) page 11*

"You should pay special attention to the different ways in which the left hand makes the accompaniment: as syncopated rhythm in some passages, answering to the melody in others, and being part of the melody in itself."

2. Don't Kill Me or I'll Die *(Milongo) page 15*

"The Milonga has a typical rhythmical structure that gives a sense of continuity when being played. In order to get this, it has to be played with the right accentuation:

It is worth noticing that although improvisation is not usual in traditional tango –as in jazz music, for example- , we tend to "improvise" variations on the main part. In this tune we have a typical variation as part B."

3. My Friend *(Tango) page 17*

"In this example, the right hand plays only the melodic line, leaving the accompaniment to the left hand. Note the use of *staccato* quarter notes for the introduction."

4. Without Realizing It *(Tango) page 19*

"In the musical style known as tango-song, the accompaniment is rhythmically less stressed, the harmony does not follow the usual changes and the tempo is generally slower than in traditional tango. In this example, we should keep in mind not only the *rubato* at the beginning of the(pick-up bar) but also the pedal note, which is a very popular resource for endings: in this example in beats 2 and 4."

5. Two Words *(Waltz) page 23*

"Waltz underlines the fact that tango is a piece for dancing. Therefore, it is essential to keep the tempo. Although the left hand is playing eighth notes, we have to keep the accentuation on the beat number 1."

6. *Blanca*   *(Waltz) page 25*

"Once again, the left hand is accompanying in different ways: syncopated, four (quarter notes), with the rhythm of the melody. Note also the harmonized melody (known in jazz music as bloque or seccional). This tango ends with part of the melody of "Adiós Nonino" by Astor Piazzolla, as a quotation."

7. *Headache*   *(Milongo) page 27*

"Contrasting to the previous milonga, this one was written using bigger figures, to make the reading easier, because the tempo is faster. I this example, there should be played special attention to the counterpoint between melody and accompaniment, and also to how the left hand plays as a melodic bass as well. Once again, we have a variation on the second part, but this time played by the left hand while the right hand keeps playing the main motive. To feel more secure on playing this kind of counterpoint passages, we recommend the study of both hands separately."

8. *Queen of the Night*   *(Waltz) page 31*

"In this waltz, the left hand keeps on playing the accompaniment in half notes. We recommend this when the melodic line has a lot of rhythm."

1920's Tango Sheet Music

9. *Nobody Left in Town* *(Tango) page 35*

"Once again the left hand makes the accompaniment in different ways: syncopated, in half notes, answering to the melody with the same rhythmic structure as the melody and also, adding a new one: the 3-3-2 in bar number 35:

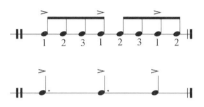

10. *Nothing to Lose* *(Tango) page 35*

One of the characteristics of tango music is the rubato in the melodic line, more over when it is a tango that has lyrics to be sang. The main idea is not sticking to the written part but recreating the original rhythmic structure for the accompaniment and for the melody. In some cases, it is better to listen to a recorded example, because the written parts are not the same as the way they are played. In this tango, we suggest changing the rhythm of the melody as in this example:

can be played

Playing this way, we will have a dissonant effect (tension) similar to the change in tempo, and finally the resolution."

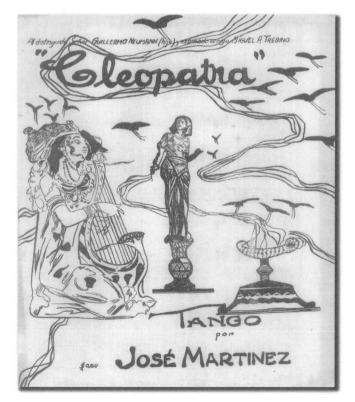

1920's Tango Sheet Music

13

The Hankerchief

Tango

Written by Jorge Polanuer

Piano

16

17

Don't Kill Me or I'll Die

Milongo

Written by Jorge Polanuer

My Friend

Tango

Written by Jorge Polanuer

Piano

Without Realizing It

Tango

Written by Jorge Polanuer

23

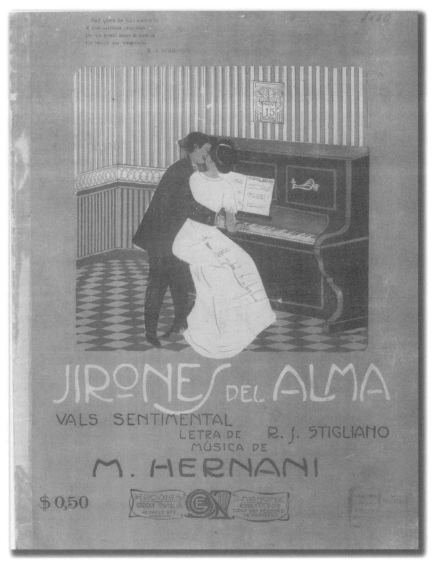

1920's Tango Sheet Music Cover

Two Words

Waltz

Written by Jorge Polanuer

♩=190

Piano

D.S. a Coda

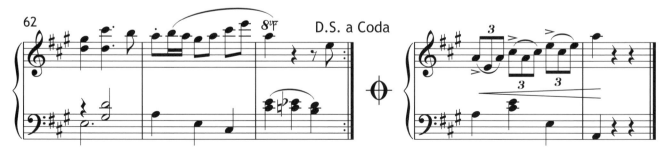

$\mathcal{B}$lanca

Tango

Written by Jorge Polanuer

27

Headache

Milongo

Music by Jorge Polanuer

1920's Tango Sheet Music

Queen of the Night

Milongo

Music by Jorge Polanuer

Piano

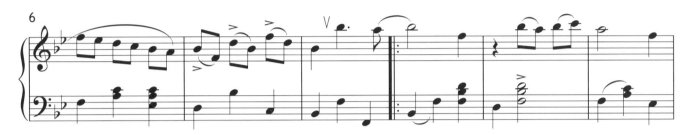

D.S. a CODA

1920's Tango Sheet Music

Nobody Left in Town

Tango

Music by Jorge Polanuer

Nothing to Lose

Tango

Music by Jorge Polanuer